POPULAR *Wedding* MUSIC
For the Advanced Player

Arranged by DAN COATES

Project Manager: Carol Cuellar
Book Cover and Design: JP Creative Group
DAN COATES® is a registered trademark of Warner Bros. Publications

Dan Coates

As a student at the University of Miami, Dan Coates paid his tuition by playing the piano at south Florida nightclubs and restaurants. One evening in 1975, after Dan had worked his unique brand of magic on the ivories, a stranger from the music field walked up and told him that he should put his inspired piano arrangements down on paper so they could be published.

Dan took the stranger's advice—and the world of music has become much richer as a result. Since that chance encounter long ago, Dan has gone on to achieve international acclaim for his brilliant piano arrangements. His Big Note, Easy Piano and Professional Touch arrangements have inspired countless piano students and established themselves as classics against which all other works must be measured.

Enjoying an exclusive association with Warner Bros. Publications since 1982, Dan has demonstrated a unique gift for writing arrangements intended for students of every level, from beginner to advanced. Dan never fails to bring a fresh and original approach to his work. Pushing his own creative boundaries with each new manuscript, he writes material that is musically exciting and educationally sound.

From the very beginning of his musical life, Dan has always been eager to seek new challenges. As a five-year-old in Syracuse, New York, he used to sneak into the home of his neighbors to play their piano. Blessed with an amazing ear for music, Dan was able to imitate the melodies of songs he had heard on the radio. Finally, his neighbors convinced his parents to buy Dan his own piano. At that point, there was no stopping his musical development. Dan won a prestigious New York State competition for music composers at the age of 15. Then, after graduating from high school, he toured the world as an arranger and pianist with the group Up With People.

Later, Dan studied piano at the University of Miami with the legendary Ivan Davis, developing his natural abilities to stylize music on the keyboard. Continuing to perform professionally during and after his college years, Dan has played the piano on national television and at the 1984 Summer Olympics in Los Angeles. He has also accompanied recording artists as diverse as Dusty Springfield and Charlotte Rae.

During his long and prolific association with Warner Bros. Publications, Dan has written many award-winning books. He conducts piano workshops worldwide, demonstrating his famous arrangements with a special spark that never fails to inspire students and teachers alike.

Contents

AMAZED

Words and Music by
MARV GREEN, AIMEE MAYO
and CHRIS LINDSEY
Arranged by DAN COATES

Slowly (♩ = 76)

(with pedal)

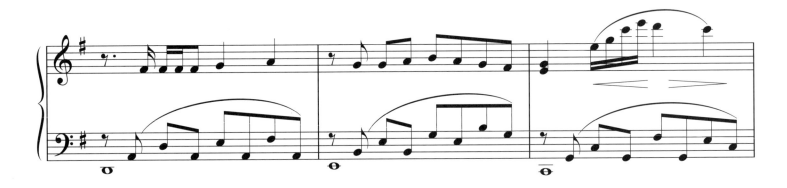

Amazed - 5 - 1

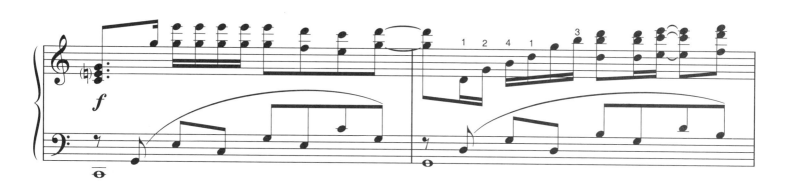

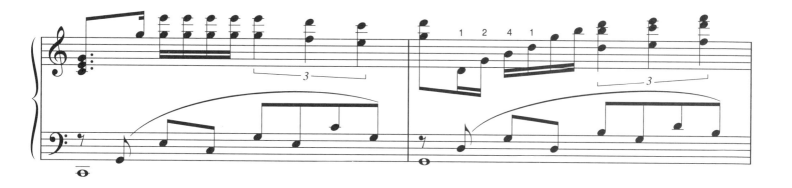

Amazed - 5 - 2

6

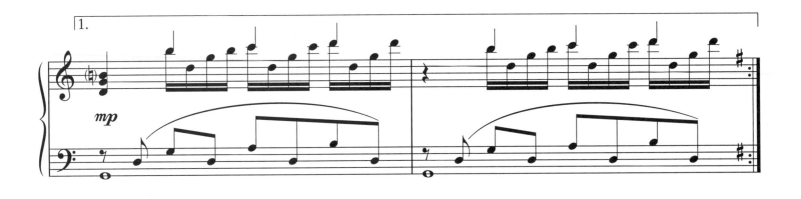

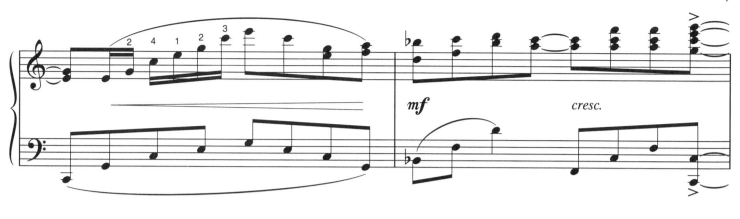

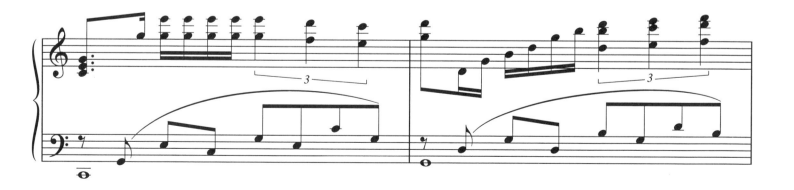

Amazed - 5 - 4

8

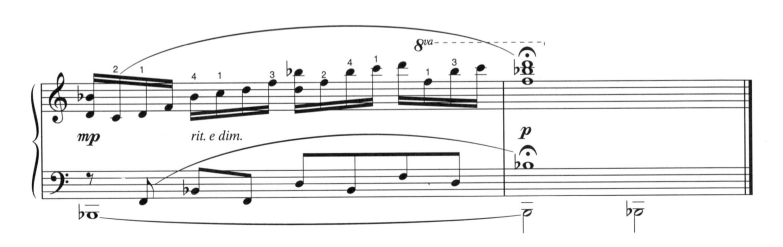

Amazed - 5 - 5

ANGEL EYES

Composed by
JIM BRICKMAN
Arranged by DAN COATES

Angel Eyes - 5 - 1

12

Angel Eyes - 5 - 5

13

AND I LOVE YOU SO

Words and Music by
DON McLEAN
Arranged by DAN COATES

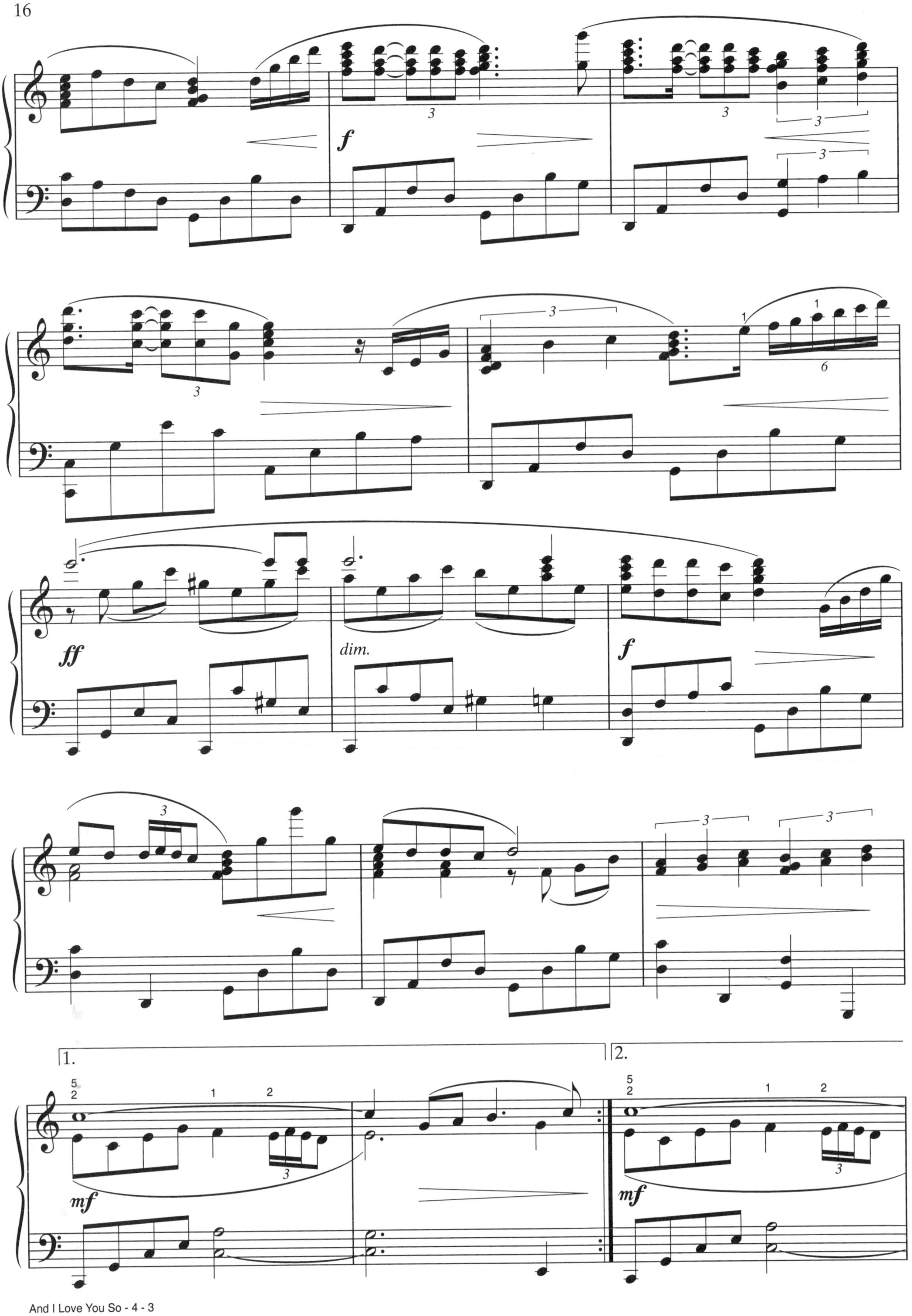

f
ff
dim.
f
1.
2.
mf
mf

Based on a Theme from the Warner Bros. TV Movie THE THORN BIRDS

ANYWHERE THE HEART GOES

(Meggie's Theme)

Words by
WILL JENNINGS

Music by
HENRY MANCINI
Arranged by DAN COATES

Anywhere the Heart Goes - 3 - 1

From the Soundtrack of the PBS Series THE CIVIL WAR, a Film by Ken Burns

ASHOKAN FAREWELL

By
JAY UNGAR
Arranged by DAN COATES

Ashokan Farewell - 3 - 1

22

AVE MARIA

FRANZ SCHUBERT, Op. 52
Arranged by DAN COATES

Ave Maria - 4 - 4

BECAUSE YOU LOVED ME
Theme from UP CLOSE & PERSONAL

Words and Music by
DIANE WARREN
Arranged by DAN COATES

Slowly (♩ = 78)

Because You Loved Me - 4 - 1

30

BRIDAL CHORUS

Music by RICHARD WAGNER
Arranged by DAN COATES

Moderato (♩ = 72)

(with pedal)

Bridal Chorus - 4 - 1

Bridal Chorus - 4 - 2

Bridal Chorus - 4 - 4

From the Broadway Musical Production BARNUM
THE COLORS OF MY LIFE

Music by
CY COLEMAN

Lyrics by
MICHAEL STEWART
Arranged by DAN COATES

The Colors of My Life - 4 - 1

COULD I HAVE THIS DANCE?

Words and Music by
BOB HOUSE and WAYLAND HOLYFIELD
Arranged by DAN COATES

Could I Have This Dance? - 3 - 1

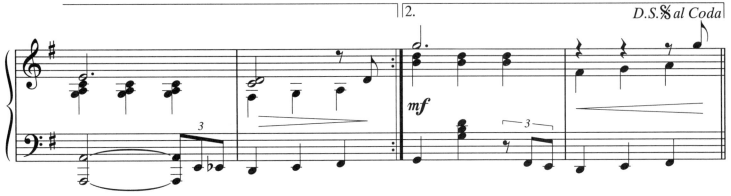

ENDLESS LOVE

Words and Music by
LIONEL RICHIE
Arranged by DAN COATES

Moderately slow (♩ = 96)

Endless Love - 5 - 1

44

Endless Love - 5 - 2

46

EVERGREEN
Love Theme from "A Star Is Born"

Words by
PAUL WILLIAMS

Music by
BARBRA STREISAND
Arranged by DAN COATES

Evergreen - 6 - 1

50

52

FROM THIS MOMENT ON

Words and Music by
SHANIA TWAIN and R.J. LANGE
Arranged by DAN COATES

Slowly (♩ = 72)

mf *legato*

(with pedal throughout)

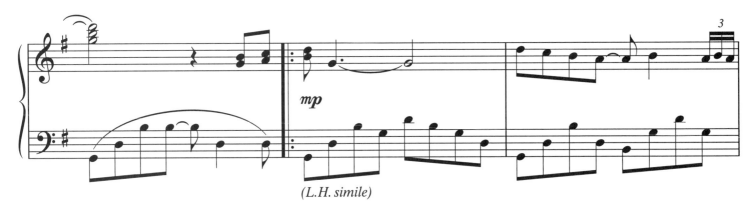

(L.H. simile)

From This Moment On - 4 - 1

THE GREATEST LOVE OF ALL

Words by
LINDA CREED

Music by
MICHAEL MASSER
Arranged by DAN COATES

Rubato

Slowly, with feeling

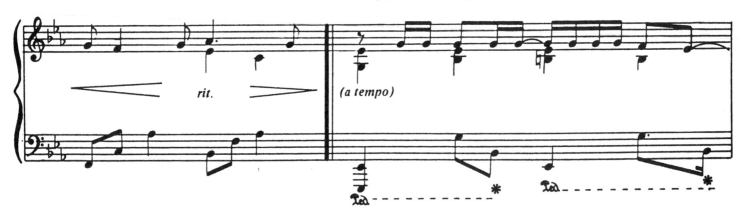

The Greatest Love of All - 5 - 1

(EVERYTHING I DO) I DO IT FOR YOU

Lyrics and Music by
BRYAN ADAMS, R.J. LANGE
and M. KAMEN
Arranged by DAN COATES

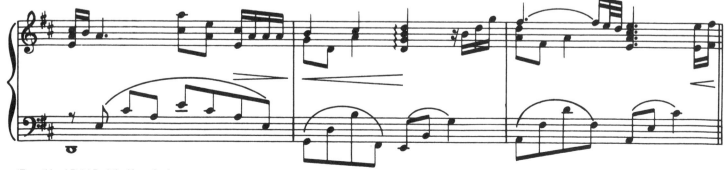

(Everything I Do) I Do It for You - 3 - 1

64

(Everything I Do) I Do It for You - 3 - 2

65

(Everything I Do) I Do It for You - 3 - 3

THE HOMECOMING

By
HAGOOD HARDY
Arranged by DAN COATES

Moderately slow, with expression

(with pedal throughout)

The Homecoming - 4 - 1

I BELIEVE

Words and Music by
**ERWIN DRAKE, IRVIN GRAHAM,
JIMMY SHIRL and AL STILLMAN**
Arranged by DAN COATES

I Believe - 4 - 1

I Believe - 4 - 2

I SWEAR

Words and Music by
GARY BAKER and FRANK MYERS
Arranged by DAN COATES

I Swear - 4 - 1

I Swear - 4 - 2

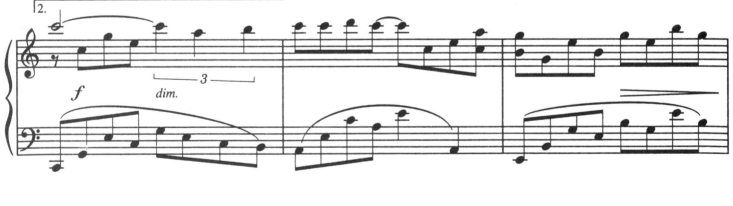

I WILL ALWAYS LOVE YOU

Words and Music by
DOLLY PARTON
Arranged by DAN COATES

I Will Always Love You - 4 - 1

80

I Will Always Love You - 4 - 3

LOVE SOLO

Music by
DAN COATES

Moderately slow, with expression

Love Solo - 3 - 1

84

A LOVE UNTIL
THE END OF TIME

By
CAROL CONNORS
and LEE HOLDRIDGE
Arranged by DAN COATES

A Love Until the End of Time - 3 - 1

From the Motion Picture THE WIZARD OF OZ

OVER THE RAINBOW

Lyric by
E.Y. HARBURG

Music by
HAROLD ARLEN
Arranged by DAN COATES

Over the Rainbow - 6 - 1

90

Over the Rainbow - 6 - 5

CANON IN D
(Pachelbel)

JOHANN PACHELBEL (1653-1706)
Arranged by DAN COATES

Canon in D - 4 - 1

Canon in D - 4 - 2

Canon in D - 4 - 4

THE PRAYER

Words and Music by
CAROLE BAYER SAGER and DAVID FOSTER
Arranged by DAN COATES

Slowly, with expression (♩ = 84)

The Prayer - 4 - 1

The Prayer - 4 - 2

The Prayer - 4 - 4

SOMEWHERE IN TIME

By JOHN BARRY
Arranged by DAN COATES

Moderately slow, with expression

Somewhere in Time - 4 - 1

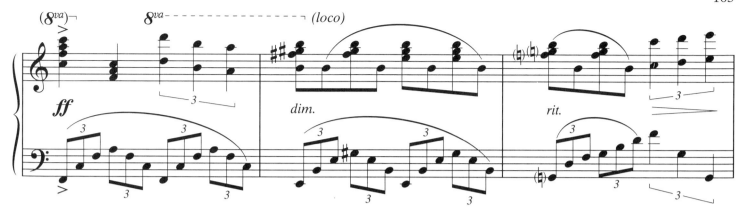

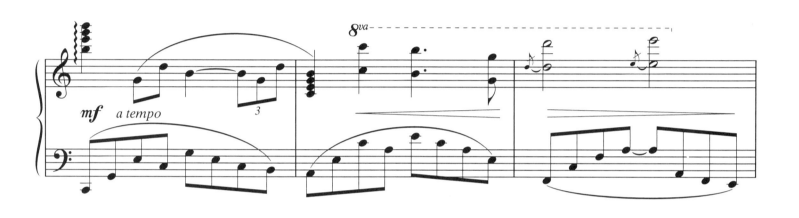

SOMEWHERE OUT THERE

Words and Music by
JAMES HORNER, BARRY MANN
and CYNTHIA WEIL
Arranged by DAN COATES

Moderately slow, with expression

Somewhere Out There - 4 - 1

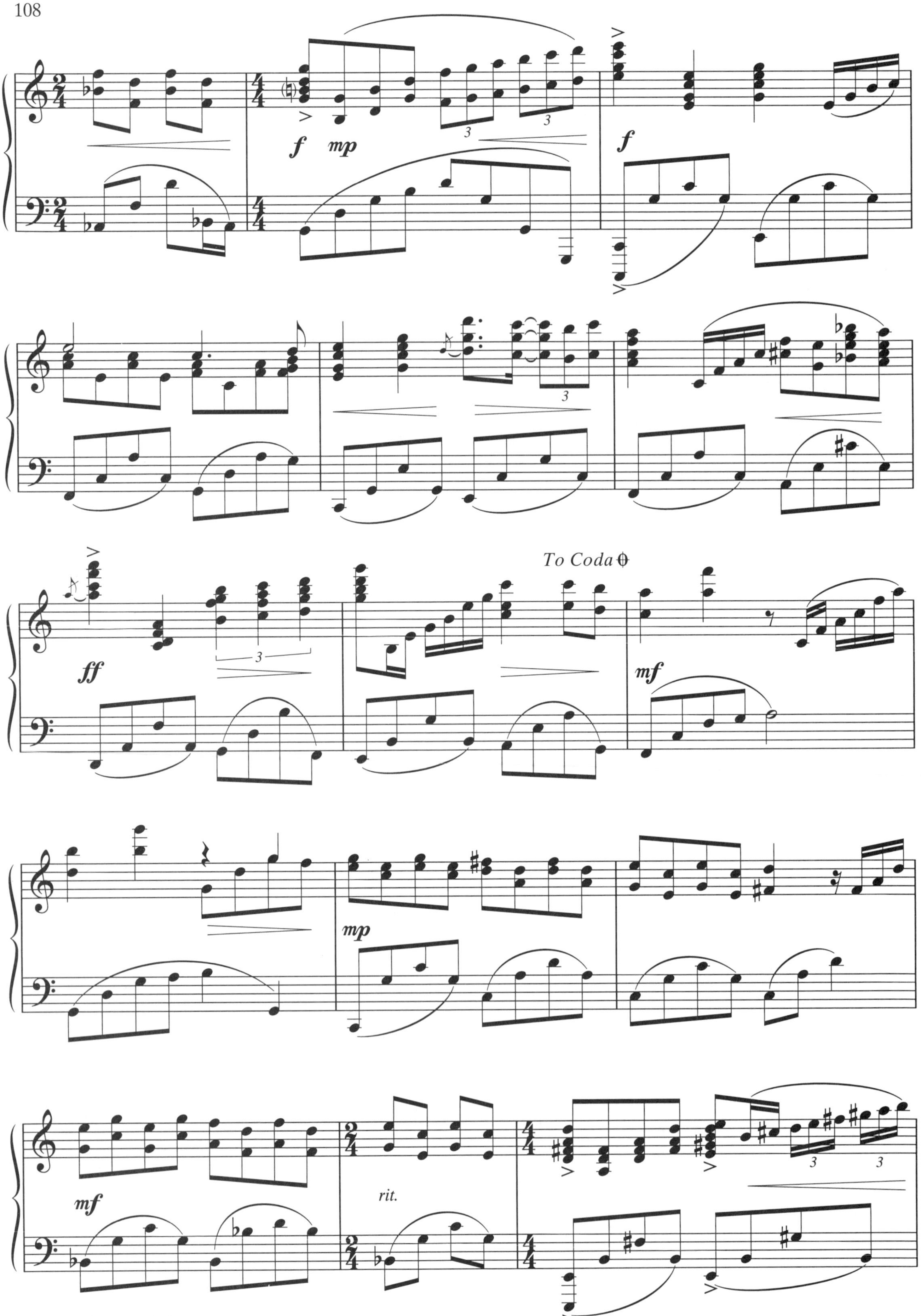
f
mp
f
ff
To Coda
mf
mp
mf
rit.

D.S. % al Coda

Coda

SUNRISE, SUNSET

Lyrics by
SHELDON HARNICK

Music by
JERRY BOCK
Arranged by DAN COATES

Moderately slow waltz

Sunrise, Sunset - 4 - 1

112

Sunrise, Sunset - 4 - 3

Sunrise, Sunset - 4 - 4

THEME FROM ICE CASTLES
(Through the Eyes of Love)

Lyrics by
CAROLE BAYER SAGER

Music by
MARVIN HAMLISCH
Arranged by DAN COATES

Slowly, with feeling

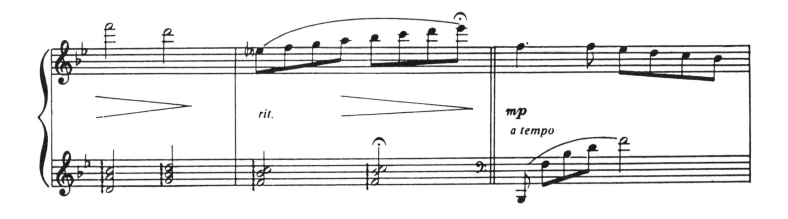

Theme From Ice Castles - 4 - 1

TONIGHT I CELEBRATE MY LOVE

Words and Music by
MICHAEL MASSER and GERRY GOFFIN
Arranged by DAN COATES

Moderately Slow (♩ = 60)

Tonight I Celebrate My Love - 3 - 1

Tonight I Celebrate My Love - 3 - 2

TRUE LOVE

Words and Music by
COLE PORTER
Arranged by DAN COATES

Moderately slow waltz (♩ = 96)

True Love - 5 - 1

122

From the Motion Picture AN OFFICER AND A GENTLEMAN

UP WHERE WE BELONG

Words by
WILL JENNINGS

Music by
JACK NITZSCHE and
BUFFY SAINTE-MARIE
Arranged by DAN COATES

Moderately Slow (♩ = 69)

Up Where We Belong - 3 - 1

128

THE WEDDING MARCH

By FELIX MENDELSSOHN
Arranged by DAN COATES

Allegro (♩ = 128)

The Wedding March - 5 - 1

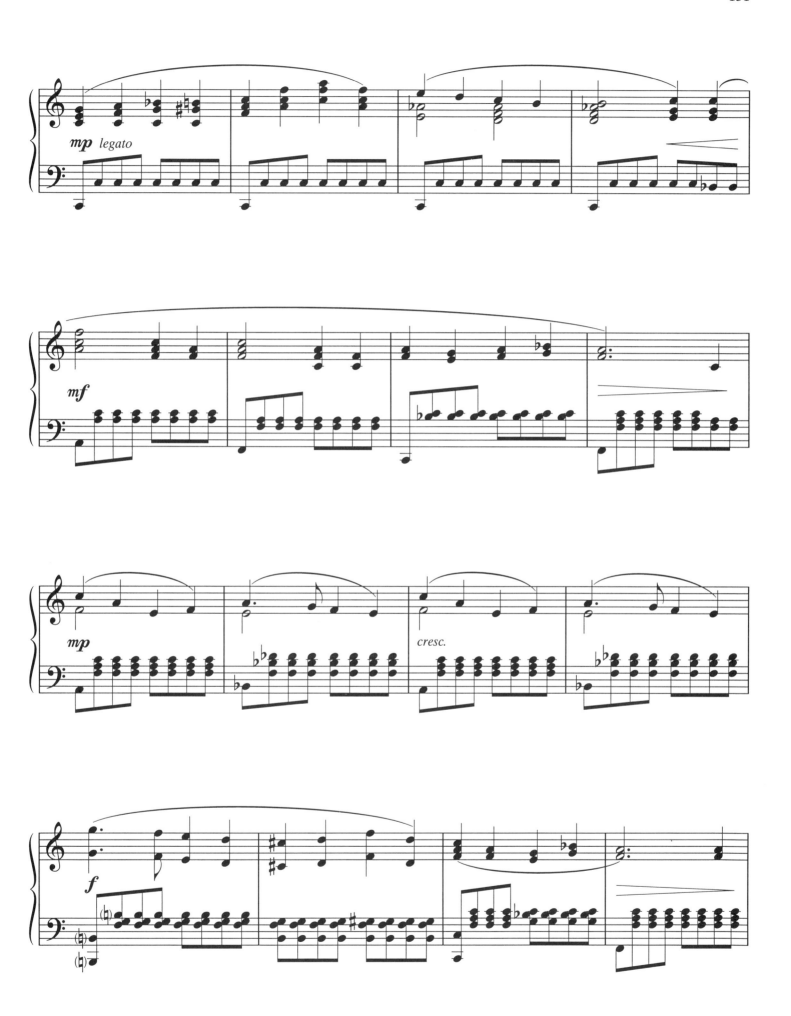

The Wedding March - 5 - 5

VALENTINE

Composed by
JIM BRICKMAN and JACK KUGELL
Arranged by DAN COATES

Valentine - 4 - 1

Valentine - 4 - 4

WITH YOU IN MIND

By DAN COATES

Slowly, with expression

With You in Mind - 4 - 4

YOU NEEDED ME

Words and Music by
RANDY GOODRUM
Arranged by DAN COATES

You Needed Me - 4 - 1

From the Original Motion Picture Soundtrack BEACHES

THE WIND BENEATH MY WINGS

Words and Music by
LARRY HENLEY and JEFF SILBAR
Arranged by DAN COATES

The Wind Beneath My Wings - 3 - 1